Brad Pitt

NANCY TAYLOR

Level 2

Series Editors: Andy Hopkins and Jocelyn Potter

Pearson Education Limited
Edinburgh Gate, Harlow,
Essex CM20 2JE, England
and Associated Companies throughout the world.

ISBN 0 582 40830 X

First published 2000

Typeset by Digital Type, London
Set in 11/14pt Bembo
Printed in Spain by Mateu Cromo, S. A. Pinto (Madrid)

Published by Pearson Education Limited in association with
Penguin Books Ltd, both companies being subsidiaries of Pearson Plc

Acknowledgments:
All Action: pp. iv, vi, and 19; Aquarius Library: pp. 5, 11, 12, and 14; Retna: p. 6;
The Kobal Collection: pp. 9, 15, and 17; Rex Features: p. 21

Every effort has been made to trace copyright holders in every case.
The publishers would be interested to hear from any not acknowledged here.

For a complete list of the titles available in the Penguin Readers series please write to your local
Pearson Education office or to: Marketing Department, Penguin Longman Publishing,
5 Bentinck Street, London W1M 5RN.

Contents

Is the real Brad Pitt crazy, dangerous, angry, and sexy?

Introduction

Brad always liked good movies with strong stories and strong acting. He didn't plan to be an actor when he was a teenager. But movies put new ideas in his head.

Brad Pitt doesn't like to talk to newspaper people. He doesn't like to answer their questions about his life. He smiles and asks *them* questions. He told *Rolling Stone* magazine, "I don't want people to know me. I don't know anything about my favorite actors."

People see Brad Pitt and they don't forget him. Before he was famous, one director says, "It was exciting when Brad walked into a room. The camera loved him." His early acting teacher says, "When Brad smiled, people remembered his face."

And people want to know *more* about Brad Pitt. He's rich and famous: he can ask $20,000,000 for a movie. He's beautiful and sexy. Dustin Hoffman says that, next to Brad Pitt, other men are as good-looking as vegetables. And, he's different from most movie stars. Everybody says he's really nice! People like Brad Pitt when they talk to him. They like him when they work with him. When people see him in a movie, they fall in love with him. They want his picture on their bedroom wall, they want him to be their friend. They want to know everything about "the real Brad Pitt."

We know Brad Pitt from his movies. He was crazy in *Twelve Monkeys* and *True Romance*. He was dangerous in *Too Young to Die?* and *Kalifornia*. He was angry in *Sleepers* and *The Devil's Own*. And he was sexy in *Thelma and Louise*. He wants to try different things in each movie. But is the real Brad Pitt crazy, dangerous, angry, and sexy?

Brad was one of many nice, intelligent teenagers at Kickapoo High School.

Chapter 1   Where Did He Come From?

Brad was born in Oklahoma on December 18, 1963. He has his father's name, William Bradley Pitt, but everybody always called him Brad. The family moved to Springfield, Missouri, when Brad was a baby. His parents and his brother and sister all live in Springfield today. Brad loves his parents and listens to them. He built a house near Springfield and goes there often.

When Brad was a child, his parents helped him in many ways. They worked hard and took the children to church every Sunday. Mr. Pitt also took his sons and daughter on trips with him in their school vacations. The children loved these trips and had a wonderful time with their dad.

Brad remembers an important tennis game when he was young. He got really angry. He shouted and kicked the ball. His father asked him about tennis: "Is this fun for you?"

Brad shouted, "No, it isn't."

Brad's father looked at him and said, "Then don't do it." Brad learned a big lesson from this conversation with his dad. He thinks about it when he does new things in his life.

At school, Brad was interested in everything: music, sports, theater, writing, and girls. He was one of many nice, intelligent teenagers at Kickapoo High School. His future looked good, but not very exciting. But his brother says that Brad was always "different."

One difference was The Brief Boys. Brad and three other boys in his high school sang funny songs. And they didn't wear their shirts or jeans. The girls loved Brad without his shirt. He had a friendly smile, wonderful blue eyes, and a beautiful body.

Brad's life was also different because girls followed him everywhere. His first serious love was Sara Hart, a girl from a different high school. After he met her, he wrote her a note in the snow outside of her house. The note said, "Hi, Sara" in big letters. They dated for a long time in high school, but they never planned to marry. They saw a great big world out there for them.

Brad got some of his ideas about a bigger world from movies and music. In the 1960s he liked *Planet of the Apes* and *Butch Cassidy and the Sundance Kid*. In the 1970s one of his favorite movies was *Saturday Night Fever*. He liked it because it showed a faster, dirtier, and more exciting world than Springfield. He liked good movies with strong stories and strong acting. He didn't plan to be an actor when he was a teenager. But movies put new ideas in his head.

Chapter 2   College Days

After high school, Brad's next stop was the University of Missouri. His dad gave him an old car, and Brad drove the 240 kilometers to the university in September 1982. Again, Brad was a good student. But he says that his favorite class at college was "fun."

In his first year at college, Brad and some friends were in a show. The money from the tickets was for sick children. The boys sang and danced. Then they took off their clothes. The theater was full. There were girls on every chair, on the floor, and on the stairs. They wanted to see Brad Pitt without any clothes. Brad smiled—this was fun!

Brad was serious sometimes, too. He thought about the lessons from church. But he stopped going there every Sunday. He felt sad because church was important to his family. But Brad was ready for some different ideas.

One evening, Brad and some college friends were in his old

car. They had a serious accident. The top of the car came off, but Brad and his friends were OK. After the accident, Brad thought carefully about his future. From that day *he* planned his life.

Brad's life changed again two weeks before the end of his classes at the University of Missouri. He walked out. He didn't finish his classes, and he didn't write his last two papers. He learned a lot of things in four years at college, but now he wanted to learn about real life.

Brad put his things in his car, and he left college with $325. He didn't want a job in an office and he didn't want to feel bored. He was twenty-two years old and ready for life in the big world. He left Missouri and drove west to Hollywood. He planned to be an actor in one year.

Chapter 3   A Different America?

The drive across America was fun for Brad. At each new state, he got more and more excited. He was on his way to Hollywood! But in Los Angeles Brad went into a MacDonald's hamburger place and thought, "Is this it?" Nothing looked exciting or different. Was he in the wrong place?

We know that this was the *right* place for Brad. Slowly he started to understand Hollywood. He worked at his first jobs for very little money. He drove a car for dancers. He sold things by telephone. He gave away free cigarettes to people on the street. But his favorite job was his first "acting" job. He was the big yellow chicken for the Pollo Loco restaurant. He stood outside of the restaurant and jumped up and down. He had fun and got $9 an hour for his "acting."

Brad paid for food, for acting lessons, and for an apartment. He lived with seven other young men. Brad said, "There were two of us in the back room, two in the other little room, four in the living-room. No beds or chairs. We had a telephone, a bathroom, and a little kitchen. We slept on the floor."

Brad worked hard with his acting teacher for months. Then he got a very small role in a TV program. In his first role, he didn't say anything. In his second, he said one word. He called his parents when he got his first important role on one of the biggest programs in the 1980s, *Dallas*. He told them, "I'm not a student here in Los Angeles—I'm an actor!" "I knew it!" said his father.

Everybody watched *Dallas* in 1987. And everybody saw Brad on it for five weeks. He played a good-looking but not very intelligent teenager. (He was twenty-three years old at the time.) It wasn't an interesting or difficult role, but more and more girls fell in love with him.

Chapter 4   Acting: The Early Years

Things began to happen quickly for Brad after *Dallas*. He had roles in TV programs: *Head of the Class* (1988), *21 Jump Street* (1988, with Johnny Depp), and *thirtysomething* (1989). He had work in movies, too: *A Stoning in Fulham County* (1988), *Across the Tracks* (1991), and other film work.

Brad learned more about acting from every role. He also often found a new girlfriend when he got a new job. He fell in love easily. He dated Shalane McCall from *Dallas* for two months. Shalane says, "I loved Brad more than anything in the world." At the end of their romance, Shalane cried for three days. He dated Robin Givens from *Head of the Class* for six months.

Robin Givens was the wife of a famous fighter, Mike Tyson, before she met Brad. One night, Mike Tyson came to Robin's house. Brad was there, and Tyson was not happy about that. Robin did not want Tyson to hit the prettiest face in Hollywood. Brad went home early that evening.

Things began to happen quickly for Brad after Dallas.

Brad also made a TV advertisement in 1988 for Levi's Jeans.

Brad also made a TV advertisement in 1988 for Levi's Jeans. This was an important job because women in Europe saw Brad without a shirt for the first time. They wanted to see more of the "Levi's Jeans boy" with the sexy smile and beautiful body.

Brad learned a lot about life, too, in his first four years in Los Angeles. He carried a notebook with him when he worked on TV programs or movies. He liked to do pictures of buildings. He also studied and read in his free time. But he wanted more. He wanted an important role in a movie and a serious girlfriend. He found these things when he made *Too Young to Die?*, a TV movie, in 1990.

Too Young to Die? tells the story of Amanda, a teenager with a lot of problems in her life. She has a crazy boyfriend, Billy. He sells her to other men for sex. He says that she has to kill somebody. Juliette Lewis was Amanda and Brad Pitt was Billy. She was much younger than him, and they were great in this serious movie. Brad didn't look beautiful. His body was thin, and he looked hungry and dangerous. But he was real, and people were really interested in him.

After they finished their work on *Too Young to Die?*, Brad and Juliette were good friends. They drove round in Brad's car. They listened to music and watched movies. Brad really liked Juliette, but their romance started slowly. Juliette was only sixteen years old.

But she was also *the* woman for Brad. They moved into a house and had fun. Juliette learned to cook, and Brad taught her about music. They loved reading and had one room in their house for their books. They liked animals, too. Brad had three dogs and Juliette had a cat. Brad stayed with Juliette for three years. She was the center of his life.

Chapter 5 The Right Role

After *Too Young to Die?* Brad and Juliette made two important movies. Juliette went to Florida for *Cape Fear* with Robert DeNiro. In June 1990, Brad began work on *Thelma and Louise*.

The director of *Thelma and Louise* was Ridley Scott. Early in 1990, Brad and 400 other young actors went to Ridley Scott's office and read the role of "J. D." with Geena Davis, one of the stars of the movie. It was a small but important role. Brad understood this kind of man. J. D. was sexy and he liked women. He was from Oklahoma and he wasn't serious. But Ridley Scott wanted Billy Baldwin for the role. Then suddenly, Billy Baldwin had a bigger role in a different movie, *Backdraft* (1991). He couldn't do *Thelma and Louise*, so Ridley Scott called Brad Pitt. Brad was the new J. D., and he was on his way to the top.

Thelma and Louise tells the story of two women. They leave home one day for a fishing vacation. They have problems on the first night, and Louise (Susan Sarandon) kills a man. They run from the police and meet J. D. on the road. With his smile and his body, Brad Pitt lights up the movie. He wins Thelma's love in about two minutes. He stays with her for one sexy night and changes her life. In the morning, she has the biggest smile in the world on her face. Then J. D. leaves quietly with Thelma and Louise's money. One night of love costs the women $6,600.

Brad was in *Thelma and Louise* for fourteen minutes, but now he was a star. Everybody on the movie says that Brad was friendly, nice, and fun. Brad loved "working with all those great people." He says, "It's the same as in tennis. When you play with a great player, your game gets better." But he had one problem: What did his mother think about him and Geena Davis in the same bed?

Thelma and Louise was a really big movie in 1991. Juliette Lewis saw it with Brad. She said, "Everybody shouted, 'Brad! Brad! Over here!' It was crazy." They all wanted him.

J. D. wins Thelma's love in about two minutes.

Another teenage girl saw *Thelma and Louise* in 1991 and loved it, too. Her name? Gwyneth Paltrow. She met Brad three years later, and something interesting happened.

Chapter 6   Life After "J. D."

After five years in Hollywood, Brad was famous. Directors wanted him in all kinds of movies, but they wanted another J. D. Brad wanted different roles. He always says, "I want my work to stay interesting." His next three movies were all very different from *Thelma and Louise*. One of them, *The Favor*, was a mistake. It was a weak romantic story, and not many people saw it.

Then Brad starred in *Johnny Suede*. He was a strange, sad musician. Every day, Brad sat in a chair for two hours before his hair was ready. The movie won some awards, but not many people saw it. Brad says, "I like it, but my parents hated it." It was a strange movie for them.

Next, he made *Cool World* with Kim Basinger. It was an interesting idea, but it didn't work. After these three movies, Brad had to be in another *big* movie. His next job changed him from an interesting little star from Missouri to a great big Hollywood star.

A River Runs Through It is a big, beautiful movie, and it has a famous director, Robert Redford. Brad played the role of Paul. He is the younger, wilder brother in the movie. He is smart and good-looking on the outside, but he is sad and dangerous on the inside.

Brad learned to fish for this role. He learned on the top of tall buildings in Hollywood and in his friends' swimming pools. Then he went to Montana and fished in a real river.

A River Runs Through It was good for Brad. He learned a lot from Redford and enjoyed working with him. Most of the newspapers liked Brad in the movie, and it made a lot of money.

Then Brad starred in Johnny Suede.

But Brad wasn't happy with everything about it. Paul looked weak and too pretty. He was always in the sun, with beautiful hair, and a big smile. For Brad, Paul had more inside, but the movie didn't show this.

Chapter 7   Two Strange Roles

Between 1993 and 1995, Brad Pitt made six important movies. Some of them were important because a lot of people saw them. All of them were important because they were intelligent movies. He was famous after *Thelma and Louise* and *A River Runs Through It*, but his feet stayed on the ground. He thought about his new movies and took the difficult, interesting roles.

In 1993, Brad and Juliette Lewis lived in the same house, and

Brad plays Early Grayce, a crazy, bad killer.

they wanted to work together again. They were excited when director Dominic Sena wanted them for his movie, *Kalifornia* (1993). They had the two most difficult roles. "I asked for it," says Brad. "You take a movie because it's hard. Not because it's easy or the same as before."

Brad plays Early Grayce, a crazy, bad killer and Juliette is his waitress girlfriend, Adele. Brad looks almost ugly in this role. He has long, dark, dirty hair, and he wears dirty T-shirts and old pants. Brad and Juliette were good in *Kalifornia*, but the movie didn't make much money. Brad says, "I went to bed one night and it was in the movie theaters. I got up the next morning and it wasn't there!" Maybe the story was too depressing for most Americans.

In his next movie, *True Romance*, Brad had a small but important role. Brad liked *True Romance* because Quentin Tarantino wrote the story for it. After Tarantino's movie, *Reservoir Dogs*, everybody in Hollywood wanted to work with him. Brad plays Floyd, the strange friend of Christian Slater, the star of the movie. He has long hair and a sleepy look on his face. He lives in front of the TV and says the wrong things to the wrong people. This makes problems for his friend.

Brad finished *True Romance* in February 1993. At the same time, he ended his romance with Juliette Lewis. After three happy years, she wanted to marry Brad, but he wasn't ready. He loved Juliette, but he moved out of their house. He couldn't be as serious as Juliette about their future.

Brad and Juliette also had another problem. Juliette and a number of other Hollywood actors (John Travolta, Tom Cruise, Kirstie Alley) were serious about the Church of Scientology.★ This was fine for Juliette, but Brad wasn't interested.

★ Church of Scientology: L. Ron Hubbard started this new church in California in 1954. Scientologists study Hubbard's books and follow his ideas.

Chapter 8　The Jump to Superstar

After *True Romance*, two movies pushed Brad from "star" to "superstar." First, he made *Legends of the Fall* with Anthony Hopkins. Like *A River Runs Through It*, *Legends of the Fall* is a big family story. Again, the country is beautiful, and we are in Montana. The two movies won awards for the beautiful camerawork. And again, Brad is the beautiful son with problems.

Legends made a lot of money and moved Brad into the top class of Hollywood actors. Now people bought tickets for every movie with Brad in it. Brad went to the first night with all of his family on December 25, 1994. They loved the movie. It was a great Christmas!

After *Legends*, Brad made *Interview With the Vampire*. *Interview* has great actors: Tom Cruise (Lestat), Christian Slater, Antonio

Brad made Legends of the Fall *with Anthony Hopkins.*

One newspaper story said, "Tom Cruise and Brad aren't happy together." But they were.

Banderas, and a great story by Anne Rice. But there were problems with the movie. Anne Rice didn't want Tom Cruise in the starring role. River Phoenix had an important role, but he died two weeks after filming began. Brad was very tired after *Legends*, and his role (Louis) was difficult and depressing. Brad says, "I hated doing this movie. Hated it, but I loved watching it. Louis was always sad. Five and a half months of that was too much."

One newspaper story said, "Tom Cruise and Brad aren't happy together." But they were. They had fun with their "ugly wall." They made funny faces and first Tom and then Brad took photos. Then they put the photos on their wall so everybody could see them.

When Anne Rice saw the movie, she loved it. She also loved Brad and Tom Cruise in it. She wrote about the movie in a two-page advertisement in a Hollywood newspaper. *Interview* made

$38,700,000 in the first three days in movie theaters and more than $100,000,000 from tickets in the United States.

Chapter 9   Two of Brad's Best Movies

Now Brad was a bigger star. He made a lot of money from each movie, and everybody knew his name. His face was everywhere. In 1995, *People* (a very big magazine in the United States) gave him an award. He was "The Sexiest Man in the World." And next? He made two more superstar movies.

The director, Ron Howard, wanted Brad for *Apollo 13*, but Brad wanted the role of a young detective in a much smaller movie. The name of the movie is *Seven* because it is about seven ugly days in a big, angry, loud city. Brad has to find a dangerous killer. This man kills seven people.

Brad did the dangerous running, jumping, and fighting in the movie. He ran across the tops of cars in the rain. He went through a car window and cut his arm very badly. But he didn't stop working. Everything was too exciting. The other actors in the movie were exciting, too. Morgan Freeman and Kevin Spacey had important roles, and Gwyneth Paltrow played Brad's wife. This was a small role, but she was very big in Brad's real life. She was his next serious girlfriend.

Brad met Gwyneth about two months before she got the role in *Seven*. He says, "I saw her and it was love. No question about it." Gwyneth says, "It was love. I remembered him from *Thelma and Louise*. He was beautiful in that movie. Brad is intelligent, kind, and funny. He loves his family, and he likes dogs. That's usually a good thing in people."

Seven surprised everybody. It made $13,000,000 in the movie theaters in its first weekend. It was the biggest movie in the United States in the fall of 1995.

Brad plays a young detective in Seven.

Brad Pitt also made *12 Monkeys* with Bruce Willis in 1995. Brad plays Jeffrey Goines, a sick young man in a hospital for "crazy" people. Before he began work on the movie, Brad went to a real hospital for two weeks. There, he talked to people with serious problems. He also changed his famous eyes from blue to brown. The director, Terry Gilliam, said, "Brad is crazy, funny, and wonderful in *12 Monkeys*. He's more dangerous than he looks."

12 Monkeys made a lot of money, and Brad won the Golden Globe award for his acting. After these six big movies, the future looked very exciting. Brad was one of the busiest stars in Hollywood.

Chapter 10   Life as a Superstar

In April 1995, Brad and Gwyneth went to London for the opening of *Legends of the Fall*. Everybody wanted the story about their romance and all of the newspapers wanted photos of them. Brad told the newspapers, "I am very, very happy. I'm in love."

But there were problems, too. Brad and Gwyneth had little time away from the cameras and newspaper writers. They went to the Caribbean for a vacation. They swam and sat in the sun without any clothes. When they saw their photos in newspapers and magazines everywhere, Brad felt very angry. He didn't want the world to know everything about him.

Teenage girls wrote letters to Brad about love. One said, "Dear Brad, My name is Melissa and I really love you! I have your picture on my wall, and I look at you all of the time. I hate Gwyneth. You are too good for her. Forget her! I know you really love me. Please write to me today!" Brad got tired of this kind of crazy love from strangers. He wanted the real thing with Gwyneth.

On December 18, 1995, Brad was thirty-two years old. He says, "1995 was a wonderful year." He made some strong, exciting

Brad and Gwyneth were together for two and a half years, and they planned to marry.

movies, and he met Gwyneth. After his birthday, he went to Missouri. He always goes there for Christmas with his family. That year, he took Gwyneth with him.

But before Brad and Gwyneth left for Missouri together, Brad wanted to say something important to his girlfriend. They drove to a romantic place near Hollywood. They ate and drank. They laughed together ... but then Brad got serious. He looked at Gwyneth and quietly asked the most important question: "Will you marry me?" Brad was ready, but Gwyneth wasn't. She says, "Nobody in Hollywood marries at our age and stays married." She was young and wanted to wait.

The romance between Brad and Gwyneth didn't end that Christmas. They were together for two and a half years, and they planned to marry. In 1997, they also had plans for a movie together. But something went wrong and their romance ended in June of that year. They didn't make the movie together, and Brad never talks about Gwyneth or about the end.

Chapter 11   The Real Brad

After 1996, Brad was busy as an actor, too. *Sleepers* with Robert DeNiro and Dustin Hoffman came out in 1996. *The Devil's Own* with Harrison Ford and *Seven Years in Tibet* came out in 1997. *Meet Joe Black* with Anthony Hopkins came out in 1998 and *Fight Club* followed in 1999. Some of these movies weren't as good as Brad's six movies between 1993 and 1995. The stories were weak, but each film had an interesting role for Brad. And he worked with big stars and learned from them. Brad was a superstar, too. He made $17,000,000 for his role in *Meet Joe Black*.

Brad had a new girl on his arm. He called her "my girl," but her name was Jennifer Aniston. She is Rachel on the American TV program *Friends*. Brad and Jennifer were very careful about

Brad had a new girl on his arm. Her name was Jennifer Aniston.

their romance. They didn't want their photos in the newspapers. They didn't talk to people about their life together, but they looked very happy. They liked the same things: a lot of music, quiet nights at home, fun with friends. They liked children, too. Jennifer went to Missouri and met Brad's family. He met her family, too. Brad said, "Nothing is more important than love."

The future looks interesting for Brad Pitt. He gets better-looking every year. He gets more money for each movie. He can do almost anything. One director says, "Everybody wants Brad Pitt. He's one of the biggest stars in the world today. Women love him and like him, too. And, he's a man's man. Men want to be his friend." Is the real Brad Pitt crazy, dangerous, angry, and sexy? It's a difficult question. But people say he is a little crazy, really nice, a lot of fun, intelligent, and—yes—very sexy.

And Brad? The real Brad stays out of newspapers and magazines as much as possible. He follows the right road for him. He wants to be an actor, not a star. He remembers the lessons of his mother and father. He has his feet on the ground. He enjoys every minute of his life.

ACTIVITIES

Before you read

1 How many Brad Pitt movies can you name? Do you like his movies?

2 Answer the questions. Find the words in *italics* in your dictionary.

   a Who is your *favorite* movie *actor* or *actress*?

   b What was his or her best *role* in a movie?

   c Who is the most famous film *director* in your country?

   d Who is the *sexiest* TV *star* in your country?

   e What TV *program* is he or she on?

   f Does he or she have a beautiful *body*?

   g What do *teenagers* do for *fun* in your hometown?

   h Do most *teenagers* like *serious* movies about *real* people?

   i At what age do *teenagers* begin to *date* in your country?

   j What is your *favorite advertisement* on TV?

   k Does it use *romance* and *good-looking* people?

After you read

3 Answer these questions about Brad Pitt.

   a Where does his family live?

   b How old is he now?

   c Did Brad enjoy college?

   d Why was *Dallas* an important program for Brad?

   e Why was Juliette Lewis important in his life?

   f How did *Thelma and Louise* change Brad's life?

4 Talk about Brad Pitt. What do you think?

   a How does he feel about his family?

   b Why were his early days in Hollywood fun and exciting for him?

   c Why do women always like him?

Chapters 6–11

Before you read

5 Answer the questions. Find the words in *italics* in your dictionary.

    a Name a *superstar* in:

      sports

      TV

    b Name an *award* for:

      music

      movies

    c Which things go *together*?

      Romeo   coffee   smoke   aunt   fire   uncle   Juliet   cream

    d How do you feel after a *depressing* movie?

After you read

6 Which movie is it?

    a Gwyneth Paltrow is Brad's wife.

    b Brad learns to fish.

    c Louis and Lestat are the stars.

    d Brad has a serious hair problem.

    e Brad meets Kim Basinger.

    f Brad has brown eyes.

    g Brad is in Montana for the second time.

    h It is a $17,000,000 movie for Brad.

    i Floyd loves TV.

    j Brad and Juliette Lewis star in their second movie.

Writing

7 You are a newspaper writer. You want to write a story about Brad Pitt. Write ten questions for him.

8 Write a letter to Brad Pitt. Tell him your idea for a great new movie for him.